Goodnight, Marie, May God
Have Mercy on Your Soul

Goodnight, Marie, May God Have Mercy on Your Soul

Marie Buck

ROOF BOOKS
NEW YORK

ISBN: 978-1-931824-70-5
Library of Congress Control Number: 2017932310

Cover art: Rachel Goodyear, *Mermaids*, 2009, pencil and watercolor
on paper, 84.1 x 59.4 cm. Collection of Robert Devereux, courtesy
Pippy Houldsworth Gallery, London and the artist

Cover design by Andrew Barwick

Acknowledgments
I'm grateful to the curators and editors who have hosted this work in various
forms: Josef Kaplan and Ben Fama at the Chateau; Katy Mongeau at All
Writing is Pigshit; Ben Roylance at his home; Judah Rubin at the Poetry
Project; Sara Jane Stoner and Adjua Gargi Nzinga Greaves at Segue Series;
Andrea Actis at the *Capilano Review*; Binswanger Friedman, Emily Goodman
Means, and Carl Schlachte at *a Perimeter*; Laura Henriksen at the *Recluse*; rob
mclennan at Dusie's *Tuesday Poem*; Ed Steck at *Theme Can*; Cassandra Troyan
at *Fanzine*.

Many thanks to Josef Kaplan and Steve Zultanski, who helped me revise
an early draft of the book, and to Andy Barwick, Lawrence Giffin, and
Anna Vitale for all their various help.

This book is for Aaron Winslow, Anna Vitale, and Steven Zultanski.

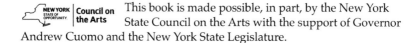 This book is made possible, in part, by the New York
State Council on the Arts with the support of Governor
Andrew Cuomo and the New York State Legislature.

Roof Books
are published by
Segue Foundation
300 Bowery, New York, NY 10012
seguefoundation.com

Roof Books
are distributed by
Small Press Distribution
1341 Seventh Street
Berkeley, CA. 94710-1403
800-869-7553 or spdbooks.org

Contents

I Hear You Drop Like a Stone

Today I hope I'll cut my hand on a drone
and get drenched in blood
and bleed out before my own vacant stare.

I'm often told "don't blink"
but I keep winking rapidly.

"Don't blink"
and yet
I wink and wink.

Lucky for me, you never know when my arm will turn
into a gun.

And yet also, you never know when my arm
will turn into an arm that shoots no one: an arm that mostly
carries, types, lifts weights, cooks, does dishes, waves hello,
and gesticulates when I talk about whatever it is I'm talking
about.

A trooper I'm looking out for wants to play
charades while still sedated.

And so I'm going to slink strangely into my chair.
My chair sits just inches away from fudge brownies,
fudge brownies that say "shut the fuck up" on them
in white icing.

I play with my keys, which hang from a lanyard;
the lanyard too says "shut the fuck up" on it.

I have a few better suggestions for the people who make
lanyards.

The lanyard would be better if it said "to have something you must own it."

Or maybe it could say:
"Real life is to be on paper, to be correct on paper.
You have to have one name, one father, one wife."

Sometimes people ask me about my worship and liegeship.
My reply remains the same:
my lord Grox is a lover, not a fighter.
That's what characterizes him.

Yet now I'm never going to be done shooting this gun.
Yet now I'm a chump and a parasite to the community.
It would be more to the point if you said
"Goodnight, Marie, may God have mercy on your soul."

Kicking Hard in My Cage

I sat there and organized my potholders.
While my father made his biscuits.
While my mother had a flower in her hair.

And my cape pulled me this way and that,
me without control,
me trying to win on my own,
me my own unhappy ruler.

In my free time, I create horses,
horses behind the house,
horses that don't look at all like horses.

I rip their images into tiny pieces.
And dip my weapon like a champion
who roams the countryside.

My soul makes a list:
I want the large iron door.
I want the glowing book.
I want the nameless.
I want to homestead on an island of nothing.
I want to dissolve.
I want to score a goal with someone else's head.
I want a big wide bed.

To make it past these ghosts, though.

Enough,
like water, leaping past those force fields, I want
sacred words, mystic gloss,
the rebels' words trapped in a box,
myself reaped from the ground into the gap,

upside-down land and water, if ghosts like
water or drivel, feet of wet clay and arms
reaching out. Opening a bottle
of champagne or two inside the flap of my little maw.
Me, a little ugly one, I drop down and sleep.

My Touch

I hold something near my ear.
I hold a paintball gun.
I hold a cup of coffee.
I hold a duffel bag and a pair of gardening shears.
I hold a cop's baton.
I keep my hand in my pocket.
I hold a knife I cut lettuce with.
I hold the steering wheel of a front-end loader.
I hold a bag.
I hold a knife.
I hold a gun.
I clench my fists.
I hold my things, which I've gathered up into my hands.

2

When you're marching, someone wishes to express solidarity,
but does not know the solidarity fist, and so first flashes a
peace sign, which is confusing in the context of this particular
protest, and then switches to pounding her heart with her
fist and then touching it with her open hand, making an
exaggerated facial expression to connote solidarity. She's at
work; she's a doorwoman at a hotel, and I wonder if she
would potentially get fired for that, were someone to put
an image of that online, were that image to go viral.

And then I wonder how I've ended up here.
Spoiling myself on the weekends
and stopping to hydrate the rest of the time.
Do I mean "sniff" or do I mean "snort"?

I want to snort,
and to deprive the powers that be of their drops of blood.

Instead I have many projects.

Do you know how to make a dog look like it's talking?
You put peanut butter in its mouth.
I know exactly how to make a dog look like it's talking.

Do I mean "sniff" or do I mean "snort"? That's like asking if
you'd rather have a real twenty bucks or a fake twenty bucks.

Today Is Tomorrow

Someday I'm going to appear
at your side

drooling.

Someday I'm going to
be as fine as gold,

a kite in the wind,
my eyes against the sun's rays.

I try to put my cigarette out
on a winter squash that's sitting

on the counter

but that feels wrong

and so not actually knowing

what else to do

I put it out by throwing it into
the bottom of your

drink
into some water with lemon

and you look at me in surprise.

"Hold your hands very still," you say.

And so I am, from then on,

in that moment,
when I make a guarantee:

in not knowing where to go,
where to ash or just how to get
myself to stop drawing so much
attention to myself

I mean, when I do that
you see a weakness
and begin to know
that I am suitable for work.

Give Up, You've Lost

Now the trees around you probably don't speak.
The history of mankind, the history of the nation
make you wish you'd never heard my name:
Old Fur-Face.

Do you want a rock to drop? I promise you
you won't hear it hit bottom.
There are great winds and mystical forces down there
in the center of the planet....

I make a soymeal and hearts of palm
casserole every night of the week.
Destiny calls me to do it.
The lights go out
and I'm in a conference room
with reporters
and flash bulbs going off
my bottom popping out of the ice
wiggling.

Someone bangs a gavel.

Me with a pudding stain on my shelf.

Me with the history of mankind

depending on what I'll do

for the next couple of hours

as someone bangs their gavel

at the bottom of the bottomless abyss.

***

I'd just like to take a break for a while.
Do something relaxing for a while.
There are too many important things to do.
It's always "study this, learn that."

For instance, I've got to hand in my paper tomorrow.
This is a term paper on King Miro.
This is not a book report on *Our Friend the Policeman*.
"Great events make great men," I write.
Did King Miro say that, you might ask.
No, I did.
I use crinkly yellow paper to write on.
I like that paper, my teacher says.

I have a dream in which Betsy Ross's
window shade is up.

I have a dream
in which my mother leaches me.

***

The whole time I was in the abyss
I had this overwhelming feeling
that my mother was protecting me
that she wanted me in her arms.
Come on, Marie, she said,
let's find ourselves a quiet spot.

But the scent of dragon is strong.

In my name
in my old name
I could sleep for a week.

Maccream
Macrack
Macarn
Macrew
You'll pay for that

I have heard my own name
whispered on the winds of knowledge.

I have felt my own wig
fluffed in the abyss.

Pick another gift, I say, or send us
to the realm of demons now.

I see it now:
from my mother's seed
all forests were born.

In my old name bottomless

my mother takes hold of my brain
and drives it to write:

We hold these truths to be...

Ugh

We hold these truths to be pretty darn clear.

No that's no good.

We hold these truths to be obvious even to a big dope.

This is so frustrating,

I feed you soymeal and hearts of palm casserole.
I leach you at the royal fish fry.

I keep hold of the big cat
and look up
at the only thing in the world
older than me.

I look into the conference room
and let myself drop into the crinkled abyss

a quiet spot
where I crack that whip.

I'm going to hide somewhere in the forest
and you have to find me.

The Price of Power

I gather up firewood.

I gather this wood up for myself.

And I'm crying for the saddest thing I know:

a wasted life.

***

When I faint I flicker,

I flicker in and out of dimensions.

When I faint I disappear.

When I faint I flicker,

unloved in my touching scene.

Tears on my knees.

A robot swimming from the doom.

***

I name myself Night Fire, Door of Shadows

and let this dark stalker prize its sash highly.

I mean I let it play dominos with a prisoner's sash

while my teacher Tongue asks,

unfurling his sponge from its sash,

Why are the whales dead?

Where have all the flowers gone?

Why are you on a roll,
eating seafood,
pollen,
grass,

while sharpening your pencil
to the ways of darkness?

Why is your darkness sputtering
in my heart of stone

when I need a constant light?

Round and round
and round and round,

my teacher Tongue shatters me
before the light.

He eats my hamburger

and glares as I set my foot
onto the dance floor.

Me, a too-wonderful babe.
Me, a creature of drool.

Tongue is chanting:
A bug flew out from under the bun!
But there's no way a bug can breathe!

Under a hamburger bun!
It would have suffocated first!
Or flown out!
When you put the ketchup on!
When you put the ketchup on!
When you put the ketchup on!
When you put the ketchup on!

***

Tongue and I share a single mind.
I call our mind "dead whale"

and let it hang there,

its blubber bouncing

and flying away.

Tongue, my custodian, my pie.
Tongue, my parent, my rash.
Tongue, your sweet embrace.
Tongue, my heart.
Tongue, my noose flapping in the wind.

I worked hard to grow
and I can't stop loving you
as I enjoy myself in this,
this doomed dimension of Hell.

A Baby Elephant Sees the Ocean for the First Time as It Quietly Dies

My teacher Tongue is my heart and soul, good God.

I drool as I stare at him.

There is only one cure that will make him well.
To have someone shed tears for him.
To have someone shed tears over his body
as it flickers in and out.

But first I'll pick the island clean.
First I'll find his dreadnought
and drink fresh cocoa fruit juice there
with the sea winds against my face.

I throw myself on the beach
and call myself "Sandy,"

my juice flavors changing, me thanking
everyone so much

and wishing I were even hungrier

while Tongue flickers in and out
and I wait to save him.

Me here, I dip myself in batter
and fry myself for a fritter,

katana and plasma cannon
while Tongue waits for me.

Stuff me with seaweed.

What a woman I am.

Stuff us both with seaweed

as I do Maneuver 36
at Octopus Cove for all to see.

Stuff me as I pull my grapple and line.

Stuff me in the cloud cover,
me splinted straight at my own self

as I lurch into adulthood at Octopus Cove.

Stuff me, stuff me! I cry.
But I cannot shed tears

over the body
of my teacher, Tongue.

10

Once I had a little competition with myself.

I was licking stickers, stickers that required licking, the way that stamps do. From a sticker book.

I thought, "I wonder how long I can hold a sticker in my mouth." I held it there on my tongue and when I felt the need to take it out I pushed through and left it there longer, breathing and swallowing without removing the sticker.

Then, not breathing, I stared at my mother, who was at the entryway to the living room, talking to my father. She didn't turn around right away, and I couldn't speak. Then she did turn around, and talked to me, and I didn't answer, and she rushed over to me, and called my father in, and I was rescued.

I Wish I Could Pass It On

I had a dream about a rich friend of mine. The friend doesn't talk about being rich, because rich people don't generally. In the dream the rich friend saw my cats multiplying, in the cat multiplying dream I often have, and he became a cat too, black and white patterned against a black and white tile floor, purring, which only further foiled my efforts to find the original cats, my cats.

No, but this is actually false. In the dream my friend was really my friend, we were marching at a protest, he said 'hey' in the voice of a sketchy twelve year old from my youth and when I looked he flashed a hundred dollar bill at me and then called me a faggot.

But in real life, I'm listening to a father explain the concept of a jingle to his daughter.

They're discussing what each of their family friends do.

And who has money and who doesn't and why.

What did you want to grow up to be when you were a child? asks the daughter.

I wanted to grow up to be your dad, says the dad. (And isn't that creepy?)

They talk about a family friend who has a house in France. And how property is cheap in France, but you have to have the time and money to fly there.

But the daughter has ideas: maybe I'll marry a pilot and then I'll live on a plane.

Okay, that's a pretty good idea.

3

When I was 8 or so, my brother and I would go over to play with some kids in our neighborhood. They were two boys, one in my grade and one in my brother's. We'd swim in their backyard pool. Their mother had forbidden them traipsing into the house when they were wet from the pool, they said, and so instead when they had to pee they illicitly peed in a cooler that sat on the back porch. They would pee in front of me on purpose and I would pretend not to care. When I had to pee, I would insist on going in the house to pee (and no one else seemed to be home or to care) and they would peer in at me through the window, since the bathroom had an open window to the back of the house. I thought I'd outsmart them and go upstairs to pee, but the upstairs bathroom window opened on to the back deck, so they had only to ascend the stairs on the back porch and they had me there too. I should have closed and locked the window. The shade was already drawn, but that is the thing they would open with their hands and look through.

Another friend of mine, a girl, claimed during sleepovers that she was not allowed to flush the toilet at night, since it woke her parents up. I would use the toilet and not flush. But the girl's solution was to pee into a hard plastic kitchen cup that she had in her room. I dared her to do it in front of me, and she did.

Later, much later, as I was friends with this girl for a long time, we went back into the creek behind her house and played in the creek itself, despite being told not to. We came back covered in mud and were stripped down in the laundry room. I was given some of the girl's clothes to wear for the rest of the day, including a pair of her underwear.

4

After I was born I had to find something to do. Sometimes I would scream into a cup. It sounded like this:

Aaaaaaaaaa.

Aaaaaaaaaa

Aaaaaaaaaaaaa

Aaaaaaaaa

Aaaaaaaaaaaaa

If You're Trying to Straighten Your Legs,
Why Do They Keep Bending

Living alone I keep a mirror in my apartment.

I see myself in the mirror every day without purposefully
looking into the mirror.

And here's one theory to try out: I keep the mirror around to
remind myself that I'm there.

Though if that doesn't make sense to you, I have a second
theory:

I keep the mirror around to trick myself into thinking another
person might be in my apartment.

I don't know which of those sounds freakier to you.

Once Someone Told Me I Had Seen the Future

For the past several weeks I've been on the verge of crying.

And so in the supermarket I buy myself something really
special,

the egg of a demon. Marked with a stamp.

Somewhere a policewoman is saving the life of a newborn
baby by breastfeeding him.

Yet here I am, crying.
Here I am, putting some moisturizer on my forehead.

I take the demon's egg from the miniature casket it's
packed in. I drop it into a pot of cool water and turn on the
flame.

I set a timer and while the egg is boiling I watch images
of women falling down over and over again. A compilation
video. Though there are things here that are subtle, subliminal
messages.

Yet I'm the one wearing the t-shirt, the t-shirt
that shows a cop, the cop with a thought bubble, oink it says,

oink, says the cop as it breastfeeds the freezing baby.

My own wrathful, sanguine hue projects itself onto the screen
and then precedes me, the pot of boiling water now has this
color too.

The egg is preparing. If this demon emerges we'll do a drug
together.

I'll stare at its breasts, its breasts like divine light, as we do acid.

We'll eat some sort of ice cream cheese dairy thing, sweating in SPD cleats at the same time. Like a really miserable experience. Like I bought this egg at the store

so I could let this other creature emerge in the shadow of me, my projected sanguine hue hitting its pot and bringing it forth, bringing it forth so that I can make it

do aerobics and eat dairy products at the same time while I stare at its breasts,

the demon a divine light, perhaps it's actually from heaven. The configurations

into which it can move its body are infinite.

There's something for everyone here. Indeed, the spiders weave their art

& the most powerful weapon on earth is the human soul on fire, says my shoe, and it's true—here I am here, eating pie.

Crinkles

It's as if when you put on those clothes you knew we'd end up
in jail.

They gave us yellow water with green stuff floating in it. And
told us we were lucky; most days you don't get the green stuff.

When I want fresh rolls, rolls hot as the sun and light as a
feather.

***

My mirror cannot see inside.

My legs, long enough to reach the ground.

My heart, big enough to touch my body's parts.

My elbow, it dances freely and hits the dissolve-o beam
at just the right angle,

so I think of us wearing our skin together,

one unit, you as my spy, me on your back,
us a disguise, my head no bigger than the rest of me

a cloak at night on the dark edge of trouble

unable to swim.

What can you hold but never touch?

I Can't Get My Ship Aloft

Even when we were out there
bunny-hopping
mad as I was—and I was hopping mad—
even then I knew.

Where hope seems lost
there rides the rebellion.
A thing of beauty
yet of this world.

Here in the Plunder Room is the energy source for the Magna Ray.
It uses the energy source of willpower. When we charge the Magna
Ray on enough willpower, we can transport them all to the Valley of
the Lost. Look at this rebel. As you can see, he has great strength of
will. The Magna Ray will be charged in no time. And afterward the
rebels make excellent servants for our generals. The strong rebel
grows weaker.

A razor-fin tore a hole in the hull.
You should have seen it swoop down.
Behold the Magna Beam Transporter.
Behold my sick wound.

Either I have a lot of guts
or I'm playing stupid.
Me, Marie, caught
with egg on my face
in this rebel brotherhood.

Me, Marie, foolishly misguided,
the last prisoner in the dungeon.
That cream's looking a little flat.
I think it needs to be whipped.

I think of taking myself into the Plunder Room
and putting myself into the Magna Ray charger.

I set the auto-reaper and go to get some food.
The tavern is closed and I ask my lady

to work on one of her magic breakfasts.

Razzle digguck
Bazzle biduck
How 'bout a big pancake?

But she just creates
a monster in the sky.
A monster that flies
and then swims.

Little people with big imaginations,
they call us.

And the time has come for you all to seek your destiny.

Unexpected Ally

What do I need for my rusty attack?
I need a pair of scissors
so I can cut off that long beautiful hair
that you like to use as a whip against me.

But the way to convert is not to attack.
I heal you. I heal you to convert you
and provide free breakfast to your children
as the light of the television flickers for me.

We could put the real thing in a cage.
We could watch him sit there.
That'd be perfect,
a disgusting little narrative

in which he tries a squeeze-play
but fails, and eventually dies
of drinking some poison
as my glaring yellow eyes

get reflected by an oil slick
and a sleepy man mumbles
angrily that his shitty landlord
should go get fucked

and so I conjure a giant holographic
version of my head.

What can we find out about this place at first light?

***

I took Annie Lennox's song "Sweet Dreams"
and replaced a bunch of lyrics to make the song actually about
cheese:

Sweet dreams are made of cheese / who am I to dis a brie, etc.

This story is a disgusting narrative in which I'm converted
from a person I dislike a little to a person I really hate, who
gets ever sadder and more neurotic.

I turn into a pair of scissors so I can cut at your long beautiful
red hair that you use as a whip against me.

I fizzle like an Alka-Seltzer and grab at a shadow.

I whisper "TV" under my breath, over and over again,
I come in like a bowlful of jelly,

I fuse together and surge through the waterfall of flame.

I Feel Like a Flat Balloon Until I See You and You Inflate Me

I try swimming through mud.
I try stopping the rain.

But here fish look like birds
and there are upside-down trees.

I mean, I'm attempting to see solid objects
but things seem to be backward here.

I'm on the beach and the beach is
bookended by giant fangs, for instance.

My mother taught me judo
but judo doesn't help you

when there's blood in the homing device.

Right now we're both a little frightened.
I light a cigarette off my forehead.

I'm Mom, I say.
And that's Dad.

Together we're a giant magnet.
I read a poem aloud:

This French dude is fucking his wife, and her clit is out of control. It's almost like this horned insect thing, and it has pincers and snips the skin at the base of his dick. And he's into it. And it exposes the flesh at the base of his dick and there's a small artery there that the pincers can snip so that he bleeds. And I looked it up on Wikipedia and it's this pleasure fetish thing.

I'm both royal guard and royal gardener,
my noose is the space debris that collects at garden's edge.

But I was born with my own perfect, egg-white shadow
of a smaller version of myself along the side of my body.

Here we arrive at the end:
the three-pronged symbol of peace.

King Kevin Begins to Worship Loop and
I Try Not to Care

We have visitors?
Let's insist they stay.
The visitors are popular figures;
they insist on hearing the story of Loop.

Loop the Maniac, Loop, maniac of Night Sky,
Loop the Years-Brat, Loop, meaningless spindle,
Loop, orchestrator of cyclists' minds, Loop the Shaven Thigh.
It's his very dipper, I say

that allows us our breaths.
Yet we need an intervention
when we get caught sowing his seed,
permissionless.

And pensionless,
blessed with ecstasies only,
spaniels bleating and
Loop washing the dead whale

up to shore
with a little nip of his breath
just touching
the surface.

Loop's beauty is grotesque:
eye sockets of Venetian blinds
caked in blood,
hamburger in his hand,

some icy froth
at the base of his neck,

a pink ridge
streaming a blue fluid

on the nose
at the center
of his
humped face.

We have visitors?
Let's insist they stay.
No really.
Let's insist.

Loop himself defines illness.
Loop himself lips our cheeks
and these visitors must know something
of this sick world, which

penetrates our ears
with the gentlest touch.
King Kevin,
King Kevin

sits on the jowls of his own
face
on the toilet under
the reliquary.

He burns eggs and
smashes the flame.
He wiggles his toes
and smashes his cans,

yolk on his own face
I mean his face is
disgusting now.

King Kevin worships Loop,
licks a child's eyelid
and shuts himself into the bloated
wires. He sticks an icee down his shirt.

Sooner or later his nose will explode
and the shrapnel
is liable to hit a child.
A rude, dumb, innocent child

whose alma mater looks
beautiful in the snow
and whose gun-wielding hands
temporarily reanimate the dead.

5

Once when I was very young, perhaps five, I was playing with a friend named Elizabeth. She lived in a trailer and I remember attempting to leave the trailer for some reason, and Elizabeth locked a flimsy screen door in such a way that I couldn't get out. I have no recollection of how this was resolved. Though later that day, into the arms of Grox I fell.

Gasping & Snoring

The chain is dragged back up.

My blood runs cold.

It's time to let myself rot for a bit,

rot for one hundred years

until my diamond arrow is ready

and I'm able to steal some grain.

***

Once I sat in a smoky haze.

There was a blast of fire near my leg
and another near my temple.

Someone entered my chamber
and felt a heartbeat in the walls.

Again they entered my chamber
and felt a heart beating.

Then I banged my head against
a steel pole

while people counted my moans.
Eleven moans.

Then I took twenty-three breaths.

Should I lean my head down a bit?

6

In my dream my partner sees me walking
and interprets me as a large mechanical spider,
"Cronenbergian," he says, which mostly excites me,
as I picture two large hairy mechanical spiders licking one
another,
and the setting is never a house that fills a void but the void
itself
which is set to collect things and is therefore
mostly work emails
that you dreamt.

I Was Hoping for a Little "Marie, please don't go!"

I took pictures of my old Bunsen Burner,
I took pictures of my old locker.

I took pictures of creamed corn
and looked for a sauna
and for chicken for my lunch.

Well here I sit with some hay in my mouth.
I want you to hold me like this

with hay in my mouth
for 2000 years.

Everything atop my head
I mean my hair

is leaking into my brain
and some of my other hair is

sucking on my face.

Are you still working at the Firestone Plant?
No, I went to Princeton.

Are you still working at the Ford Plant?
No, I went to Columbia.

Are you still working at the Bosch plant?
No, I went to Yale.

And then I opened my mind to a spell
and performed torture

for money,
with my grip like a Crab-O-Saur
and my head a Tin Trespasser that goes where it wants,
a mystic vision that guides my Grabbers.

Everyone Has Seven Selves

Darkness and light
& banshee scream
& siren call

this piece of tin
won't hold me
in your puny pit.

I cock my little head to the side.

I'd be perfect to play the part
of Robert Kennedy.

A kiss on the mouth.
An exchange of flowers.

I explode
half a dozen
eggs

in
the
microwave.

I shove my
face
into your elbow

and burst
into flames.

The Public's Century

When I see another human,
I'm always like, hey cool, oh, sorry, thank you!

Eyes collect all the junk and squeeze it out the side.
But Grox, my liege, is marked on this earth by a book
  and a tooth.

This book and tooth melt the lark as it flies through the sky.
They melt the squirrel as it scurries by.

According to me, Grox nuzzles us
with book and tooth in each of our inflamed brains.
You slay me, someone giggles.
That's right. Someone is slain.

The nuzzling creates hard nubs,
nubs which can build to an apex,

and Grox whispers to these little nubs from his earth-husk.

So I guide Grox's toes to the oceanside
and hold my sports bra up with my mouth and pretend it's
  a megaphone.

I know how to make a dog look like it's talking.
You put peanut butter in its mouth.
Same goes for Grox,

so here I sit, relating to the Second Amendment.
When someone stumbles upon me like, hey cool, oh, sorry,
  thank you!
I can blow them away or tell them they're welcome.
Or I can repeat it back, hey cool, oh, sorry, thank you!

And they do it back to me, hey cool, oh, sorry, thank you!
And I'm like hey cool, oh, sorry, thank you!

Food and Blood Face

This occurred in the seaport town of Grandor.
I crawled on the sand.
Me, a multi-colored maggot.
Me, with clown make-up smeared on,
even a little tear drawn onto my face.
But a real tear washed away
the fake one.

Still today it sits on my face, refusing to run down my fat cheek.

It quivers.

There were three reports of an approaching sky intruder. And
the intruder, dissipating, blew suddenly into a purple smoke.

This isn't a saying, but a spell.
I covered my face with my wing
and finished off the dead.
I was a little drenched and then a little rotten.
Me asking my own self questions,
me taken places by a version of my own self.

I mean there are days when your arrow barely
misses my brain,
the arrow you shoot each day
as I crawl along the beach.

Knives, Tools, and Matches

Usually I get the pain right here
and I shake
like when I learned to swim
even though I was afraid of the water.

I get the pain between the dancing and the fireworks

till I vomit a golden key, violently,
onto the dance floor

and I know,

as if a little voice were telling me

where it goes,

how to get to the iron door.

Sometimes late at night I cry out your name.

And in the day my boss says,

there's gonna be a beautiful sunset tonight.
I want you to take off early to watch it.

And I say that my foot is poised at the bottom rung
of the corporate ladder.

My shoulder is to the wheel.

Do you realize how many kinds of cat toys there are?
There are the little plastic balls with the bells inside.
There are the little furry birds.

And the chew toys that remove
tartar and plaque from the teeth.

And I'm in charge of all of them.

At home I shrink the cat toys to the size of bugs.

It's the completion of the cycle,
a remarkable rain.

At work I put a catnip punching bag
up on the shelf.

I stamp the price on a box of buzzyballs.

I spray myself with a growing serum.

And I rip a whole pond out of the ground

and create a giant rainstorm

over everything.

Sweet Dreams

It's amazing
how easy it is
to take advantage
of people
who are frightened.

Our mysterious lady
talks to horses.

So our mysterious lady
talks to horses, does she?

I could clap you in chains
for that remark.

But I won't.
You speak the truth.

And I survived
the piggy pointing
his stun beam at me.

Broil me in butter
and call me flounder, I say.

That was a close one.

Here I am,

despite how hard it is
to find a decent cheeseburger
on the Crystal Isle,

despite that we took the transporter
to Beast Island on a family trip,

despite that I miss commercials
when I watch public television,

despite that I'm a patient
without an oxygen tent,

an appendicitis victim without
penicillin

out here working on my El Camino,

sweaty, grease all over my hands,

allergic to meatballs,

allergic to salad,

always having to run.

I think we have a problem
says the Sea Plunderer.
If you do not define "jock strap"
for me, I will reduce your town to rubble.

Well, the jock strap,

the jock strap,

is a particular kind of strap,

which is constructed

of a, a, strap-type material,

and which is utilized

exclusively for the purposes

of,

uh,

uhh,

yeah....

Water and Lava Inside a Closed Mountain

You peddle through the mud
like a calf, like doom,

like doom's vipers, this world that's
not your own

is like that.
I think you must dream of me

and the best you can do
is cut a sock in half

and try to create something
I'll want to have.

I know it.
I know what you're doing.

But here in the garden
at dusk

an astronaut with no training program
gets excited by me

a simple peasant girl.
You excite him too

with your gibberish
and the raw quarter pounder in your hands.

He says he's depressed and horny
on this beautiful night

and so we hear his cry:
let's place him now

on an interlocking plexiglass platform.
In front of him we stitch a quilt

where no patch is any more important
than any other patch.

Each of us takes a turn
sucking at his dick

while the other
looks steady at the horizon.

While still on our knees
we serve him steak and beer

moving about on our hands
which get a little dirty from the gravel.

He still seems depressed.
This stupid place is as good as any.

I bring out an easy-to-clean mesh screen.
I find myself missing snow-covered

streets sometimes,
my lamb-like touch

being my one
dumb address to this world.

My mesh screen
pretty useless

though,
at least against

any of the world's
known horrors.

7

Once when I was high, I came home late at night and saw a creature in a cardboard box on my front steps. I could not figure out what it was, though it was clearly living, and looking at me even, and for a moment I really truly thought that it might be an alien. Disappointingly, it was an injured baby bat that my brother had found.

12

Once I was on an inner tube in the bay.

Everyone else was on the shore. I decided to see how far out into the bay I could go, if I could make it past the buoys. I started paddling and got very far, until my mother came running into the water wearing her shorts, yelling to me and then swimming toward me, since I had gone out too far.

When we returned to the shore, Grox was there. He kissed my head and praised me and ran his scaly fingers through my salty hair. He showed my mother how far he can reach, how far his arm extends when he wants it to, how I'd never been in any danger.

I'll Pet You with My Middle Finger

Once someone told me I had seen how the sausage got made

had seen it with my computer,

which is a word I like to use for the brain.

A friend of mine does Himalayan salt lamps

and the Himalayan salt.

I remember his heat

and the promise he made to blast open the future,

and I see how nothing's been done.

How my middle finger still needs a splint,

how we ought to be thinking rocket launchers

rather than side lamps.

And yet I'm here, alone, vomiting, seeing an image of a skull

there in my vomit.

This is how my head's in a cage full of bees.

This is how I watch a close-up video of a tattoo
being created, with my head still in a cage of bees.

This guy at my gym wears a t-shirt that says
"beatings will continue until morale is improved."

And yet I'm busy noticing the freakiness of the human eyeball.
How it betrays its human's emotions and the direction of the
human's attention.

I pass before the eyeball two young dollars
and the eye follows them, as though reading across a page.

9

I had a dream the other night that I took my cats to my sweet-
heart's house to show them to my sweetheart. This sweetheart
is not my partner; he's different, and so I had to bring the cats
to him. But in this dream he already had cats there, a few of
them with different patterns cruising happily around on the
black and white tile floor of his apartment. And so I lost my
cats among his cats and could not distinguish them.

This is a variation on a dream I have much more frequently: I
am somewhere unusual with my cats. They multiply. I cannot
find the originals. The dream is a little bit different each time.

John, a friend I suppose, a casual friend with whom I am defi-
nitely out of touch now, once told me he had the same recur-
ring cat dream. John loves his cats and otherwise seems pretty
sad. I love my cats, too, but I do not think I am sad.

My friend Ashley had a dream the other night that I had a new
book coming out and wanted the cover to be an image of her
left breast in 3/4 view, including the nipple. And she thought I
was being a bit presumptuous, asking for this image to include
the nipple.

My friend Lara also dreamt of me, and this dream seems the
most accurate: in this dream I had a new book coming out, and
in my author photo I was wearing a white terrycloth bathrobe
over my clothes and sitting on a couch. Next to me was an-
other version of myself in the same outfit, but mistily transpar-
ent, like a ghost, putting an arm around the first me and
grinning.

And yet yesterday I overheard a dad explaining to his daugh-
ter the relative wealth of each of their family friends, and

where the money came from. Jingles are little songs for advertising, he says, explaining that one of their friends made his money by writing jingles in the 80s and then buying property before it became so expensive, and then selling it.

And in the morning I come across a student walking quickly next to her professor, asking if she thinks human nature is naturally bloodthirsty.

Servant & Master

Work hard, be honest, and treat others kindly,
and you'll have a happy life. —Septum Ring

All over again, she challenged me:

"See if you can reach in my pocket," she said,
"I have a little container of fat-free milk,
and I can also add a mustard packet to it."
And she challenged even me.

I'm the one who tells the past, the present, and the future.
And I, I vomit up my truths.
Hey, here's my skin
You can take it into your lungs.
Again! Again!

But I'm having a bad day
this morning
and I pull out a secret message
a little fortune I've saved:

You'll go to a restaurant
it says
There will be a coffee cup pattern on the table
your insides will drizzle out
you'll weep tears of blood
you'll lick at the air and gasp
and everyone will think you're fucked up:
I'm your only escape.

And despite my uneasy feelings
the only way we can get there is by circling in reverse
at high speed.

We've got to pull like we've never pulled before.

So everyone covers their mouths
as we ascend in the doom balloon
taking in, letting out
opening our hips
pushing our hips back over the air
and feeling it
crying while we eat
crying on all fours
crying in a fake British accent
crying while we cut them open
crying with our tongues lolling out.

I Turn a Ray into a Torch

I once watched a starfish force a microchip out of its body,
which was itself lodged in an artist's rendering of Jesus Christ.

A ridge of skin had formed around the muzzle of the starfish,
and a powerful tide began to pull on me.

I put on my leather jacket
and looked in the mirror.

Even now I hold Grox's hand and then
I hold my own face.

If the jacket had a thought it'd be,
thank you for putting me on while you're armed to the teeth
with the stolen weaponry of the fascist war machine.

But also, fuck you for mating with an officer
even if to steal a converted flame thrower.

Be mad, I instruct you.
Be mad be mad be mad be mad.

You can do exactly nothing
if you are not mad.

I put small images into each and every
coffee I taste,
and this constant evoking of my miniature selves is an art
form as old as man himself.

Do you want to sit on our stoop for a little bit and drink your milk and I'll look at a magazine.
I sink into my chair.
I think, they make train sets there.

You Know the Hole You Crawled Out From

We're living through the second gilded age,
with all that's happening to women right now.

Yeah, you fucking dick.
We're living through the second gilded age.

While doing some dental work on my mouth
my dentist asks me if I have a boyfriend?

Or a husband? And picks up my hand
to see if I'm wearing a ring.

Yeah, you fucking dick.
I do.

I came out of the birth canal
very very quickly.

So quickly
the nurse almost dropped me.

I was already wearing a t-shirt;
the t-shirt said, if it ain't pit

it ain't shit.
I already liked pit bulls.

I already liked milk.
I withdrew a small mirror

from my pocket.
And in it

I showed the nurse my
true face.

My true face is fucked up.
My tongue of that face

thrusts out for milk.
Even in a shitty, rural

town, with few opportunities
and a high crime rate,

adolescents contemplating
their futures

will say that they want to leave
and maybe come back when it's time

to have kids
since it's a good place for kids,

safer than a city
(which is untrue).

Even in rural Southern towns
where everyone speaks

with a strong Southern accent,
people still put on an exaggerated

and slightly different fake Southern accent
when they want to imitate someone

from a more rural Southern town
and suggest something bad about that person.

Yeah, you fucking dick.
You slime-filled blister.

13

Once I was at an ice-skating birthday party. It was the first time I had ever ice-skated.

I felt joyous but wrong.

I went to the bathroom and was washing my hands. I vomited suddenly and tried to swallow it, as I didn't want to be sent home, though some of it overflowed my mouth and dripped down my chin into the sink. I rinsed my mouth out. I didn't want to stop skating so I skated more.

Later my friend's Italian grandmother made us spaghetti to eat. People's parents were starting to show up and everyone praised the real Italian spaghetti.

But I was different.

After eating the spaghetti, I went down to the bathroom in the basement and threw it up. An adult came to check on me and stayed there with me in the dark patting my hair and then called my mother.

When I'd recovered a bit they brought me back up to see my friend blow out her candles. The cake showed my friend, Michelle, smiling next to Grox. Michelle didn't really look like herself, but Grox's scales and fangs were extremely realistic. "Happy Birthday, Michelle!" the cake said, in white icing.

I Serve the Void

Here is the non-discolored lump where the barbell
smashed into my hand.
You can see me here,
you see me,
you do.

In my fantasy we're at an annual festival.
But the food and beverages start
exploding. Of course, people scream.
I see it, but I can't cry and
you're all cried out, you say.

Uh-oh, the toddler exclaims,
throwing her toy to the ground.
And her mother corrects her:
you can't say uh-oh if you throw it.

That's right. And I was forced at one point to undergo a test,
a test of dreams.

In my first dream I'm wearing a sweatshirt,
it says "a woman's place is in the house
AND the senate."
And also a skirt
with a merkin
(that is, an
old-fashioned pubic
wig)
sewn onto the front,
right on top of where my
pubic hair really is.

I'm in a restaurant,
on a date with a friend of a friend,
who I really do find super hot in real life, too.
I lean across the table, I whisper to him:
I'm wearing something *very* special tonight.

And then I wake
with an overwhelming feeling of embarrassment
that I alluded to the merkin at all.
And someone is there pointing out the dried blood at key
points on my body.
Though maybe this is in the second dream.

What's so stunning about my billion-year journey?
What's so great about this trip around the sun?
I say that it's the way it's always looked like Hollywood,
this Earth so glamorous. I sparkle,

happy when I find a landline in my world,
which looks like *Lord of the Rings*.

And the second dream,
the second dream I'm not going to tell you about.
The second dream puts me in a thicket
smoking.

Hay in My Mouth for 2000 Years

I took pictures of creamed corn
and searched for a sauna.

And you drew a volleyball where my head once was
and noticed:

man is slime.

& yet I hold the key to my future in my own hands

& yet it turns out these hands are made of chicken salad
and so cannot really lift things

or even wave,
they are barely held together at all.

If I were to move these hands from my lap
I think I would find they detached from my arms, in fact.

Instead I've been given a tattooed hand
positioned so that it encircles my neck.

I'm visibly moved by it,
I know that people are watching my emotions express
themselves
since I can't really control them very well,
since I tend to get a little butter-fingered.

***

I lied, I lied, it's all lies.
The community center and its fake plants,
the hieroglyphics I wrote in, which aren't even real,
the squealing necrotic tissue that isn't really dead.

These are all fake names that I gave.
My name is actually Marie.
I've spent all of history fantasizing.
In West Germany I drank a whole bottle of vanilla flavoring.

Do you think I'm drunk?
Do you think I'm drunk?
Well, I'm drunk.

I thought I'd buy the Submission dusting powder,
but then instead I bought the Submission perfume.

I'm touching my girlfriend's skin
which is so soft it only gives me three splinters.

A blackberry thorn solders itself to my wrist-vein.
Hope is a real thing, just like despair.
I let the fish suck on my face and open my mind to that
hunk of meat.
I'm standing behind the convenience store, and I just want to
leave Earth.
But not to die,

breathe again when I've fallen into a giant pie.

Silent Friend

We met at Laughter Pond, me and a man
in a purple cloak.

First we tried to bite each other's tongues off,
it's called Dutch kissing.

Then I made him chocolate chip eggs and read
Lassie Come Home out loud to him.

I individually wrapped his chocolate for him,
I gift-wrapped two melons for him.

He touched the can opener
and talked about axe care.

And I pictured us in a ski lodge,
stone fireplace,
snowing outside,
boots by the fire.

77 cents will not do the bald eagle any good,
I said.

It will not even buy him a cap, I said.

Let me give you a little quiz.

Crabgrass: friend or foe?

Why don't gas stations give out free maps anymore?

The printing press: was it a step forward for mankind?

& he sang me the marine fight song as a lullaby.
& he took me into the slime room.
Make me laugh, he said.
"Stephanie, would you like to have some more cabernet?
I have to call my mummy."

And then he put me in the slave transport
and gave me normal kisses.

Time for me to learn what it's like
to be in a cage.

My Scalding Hoop

In the slime pit I look forward to doves of white.
Someday I'll tap a jammed box open and release them,
something to watch while I chew on tin.

Till I meet my sweet death.

But I want to blow the beast far from here
to return home and eat tofu pancakes,
couscous-based whipped cream on a sunflower cookie.

Yesterday I watched a video of my first pimple on replay.

No, life's not that hard, man.

& you're probably not going to walk into an open drainpipe,
never to come out.

Slime is wet stuff, like barf

and my coils create a sorceress's wind,

which is just what I need
to turn the tide on the multi-
colored maggot that I am.

11

Once my neighbor crashed her bike into a giant thorny bush in front of her house.

Afterward, as Grox licked her wounds, she relayed to me the story of how she had peed her pants at school earlier the same day.

I was intrigued by this and later I tried to convey it in my diary, the diary I had just begun keeping. I could not write most words yet, and so I drew a picture of her as a stick-figure wearing shorts. I drew the pee as a line coming down next to her leg.

Later that month she and I sat in the grass of her backyard in our shorts, watching her dog run around. Sitting there just by ourselves. She took off her shoe and showed me the bottom of it. There she'd written a secret word. The word was *FUCK*.

Blood-Soaked Tarot Deck

A bit like a piece of crystal
you'd stick in your armpit for luck,
that's me.

I slide out of myself like worms
and try not to think a lot of myself

but instead I keep my eye
on the sky
and fight the formations
and start-up constellations.

I bend an arm
and then the other arm.
I sit close to the television just to count the pixels
but my glasses get stuck in a tiki hut
and the tiki hut is my only on-ramp
and my face is cold and surrounded
by an ornate wreath.

I touch them.
I sound the alarm.
I break on through.

I thought my dad was just a Grateful Dead fanatic,
a bizarre form of teenage torture.
I do blink my eyes at the weird world.
I do let my entrails drag a bit, embarrassing.
I do have to ask you,
to ask you before we even get started,
when we'll be done.

My boyfriends and my dull culture and my lack of shame,
my private life and my
open-faced bid for a free dinner,
it's embarrassing.

I pray you see my signal:
I want an egg salad sandwich immediately
because tofu always tastes like nothing but tofu
no matter how good it looks.

You want to play snap the whip, eh?

Some day I'll have the power to destroy you. Some day,

if you teach me to fly the Sky Sled,
if I don't get stuck flossing
or getting stuck on a barbed wire fence
or swimming through shark-infested waters
or watching *The Sound of Music* again.

Anything made from tofu
will always completely and totally
taste like tofu.

And I know if it was embarrassing once,
it'll be embarrassing again,

my costume splitting up the middle,
anyone consulting her crystal ball
the night before a test.

Bend an arm.
Then bend the other arm.
This may be your only on-ramp
To that big information highway
in the sky.

Snap that whip.
I'm ready to jump ship.

The First Time I Ever Really Felt Safe Was Under the Weight of a Wagon Wheel

I cry and cry, for three hours
and wonder if my mount
can have a mount of its own.

Can it?
Can my creature ride another of my creatures
and bend it to its will as I
bend to my will the first of my creatures?

Right now a long hair from my head
has become trapped.

Trapped underneath the bottom of my shirt
it brushes the small of my back.

I look at my face and find my eyes:
too small.

My nose there,
with the uneven nostrils.

I relax my face muscles.
I open the file I have.

It's a file of babies meeting
their parents' twins for the first time.

Who's this? Who's this? Is that Daddy?

No.
It's not.

My own twin is standing behind the door of my bedroom
watching me.

Watching the thorny vine grow along my arteries.

I'd be better off trying to sell pre-licked food on the street.

The second part of this poem gets a little freakier:

it's a man commanding another man to rise from the dead.

The dead man *feels*, he feels a strange tugging.
A long hair from his head is trapped between the cheeks
      of his ass,
and the first feeling he has is the hair shifting slightly,
responding to some imperceptible movement he never made
because he was dead.

A shifting where he didn't expect it,
which causes him awareness.

A sharp pain in his head
makes him reach out to the man,
reach out to the man
who commands him.
The dead man lurches forward
lipping the neck of the man,
the man who commands him.

Me, though:

I'm structured to be gored
and I announce that

to the whole scene.
To the man
who commands the dead man,
to the dead man,
to the audience,
an audience that
also participates
against its own
freakish will.

I See the World Only Through My Own Shitty Eyes

The chef is busy
Sending dickwads back where they came from.
Well, there are problems in the province.
And yet I'd still like a piece of that cake.

I have to find cover and stay here,
stay in the strangest mystery, in four blue
rings with white light inside of them.
It's a white hole. Like a black hole,
but less dense.

And here I'm stuck pushing a wedge of tissue
into a big gash
my biggest gash
gagging at the sight.

I read foreign magazines
I track all of my own progress
but you'd never think I would be here.
On this doorstep.

***

The chef is busy. Well there are problems in the province. Disrupting the area. Destroying property. Think if we could turn you into a giant, brave version of yourself. I'd still like a piece of that cake.

I thank everyone for your help. And for yours and for yours. One of the mysteries—the strangest mystery—is that this is very rare, my movements on a conveyer belt succeeding, the waterfall flowing uphill.

And you know, I've longed for this moment. I clap my hands to my face and get makeup smears on them. I look at the fat knight gleaming; I'm in a dream. One current for each fluid-vessel, and the currents coming together like this is unprecedented. With the vessels stretching and reaching, me running hard and fast, the bad ones deflected, lifted, thrown out past the white blurs romping through, fluids everywhere, the dark mass tapped out as I choke on a romantic stranger's pointy tongue and toss it all to the stars. It feels as if I'm getting some sort of signal. You're a little too close for anyone's comfort, and we make you all pay.

Four blue rings with a bright light inside them. This is very rare. Don't underestimate the white hole's strength.

A Partner for My Trapeze Act

I get the Dissolve-O-Beam ready
and turn my sword into a lasso.

Last year I went to Hawaii
with my girlfriend Rena.

We ate at this Chinese restaurant,
and when they brought the fortune cookies,
hers said "you'll never amount to anything."
And so we left.

My teacher Tongue told me where the olives were
and swore we'd watch beautiful sunsets together.

But instead I put some eggplant parmesan in my handbag
and smeared it on my face
in preparation for the teargas.

Tongue has a job teaching sex ed to kids with behavior problems.

I told him I had this really dirty dream
where all I wanted was a little warmth
from the guy in the hat

who I think did something terrible,
who I think overcharged Tongue in the store

and put his voice into a voice-bubble.

Tongue didn't speak.

I feel
like a slow-toe dragging a cart, like an army

flying into the gap.

Let's hear about the cowardice and shame.
Let's use a flair to distract it.

I thought I might recite some poetry.

Tongue gives us copies of *Sports Illustrated.*
Tongue teaches us to swim
and holds a prom for the football team
in November to avoid the spring rush.

I score a goal with someone else's head.
I may chuckle.
A little guffaw.
Ha.
Ha.

These Tears I Can't Hold Inside

I'm freaking out.

The view-crystal is prepared as I ordered.

I just need somewhere to lay my head,

which is about to overflow with freedom-thoughts,

somewhere to collapse
this iron door
inside my heart

which is going to bust
and launch a dead ray.

***

The black snow falls for three days.
It ruins the crops.
It causes the animals to grow sick.

You call me Old Floppy Eyes
and make fun of my fear.

Of course there's
water in the Growling Sea,

you say,

of course there's
a weather-wheel

making black snow,
making slaves of the animals.

It takes my calculator collection,
it takes my golf clubs.

It takes my diary,
it takes my nightlight,
and spins fast as a tornado.

***

There's a stranger watching me
across the street.

He's a leach sapping my strength,
my blood.

The only way to stop him is
to get a G-U-N,

a collapsible drinking cup,
some insect repellent,
a canteen,
some electric socks.
And a G-U-N.

***

Let's see, let's see.
The magnificent one
is set to go

and tests the island's defenses.
I never thought I'd
say this to a human:

you will have the honor
of being my slave.

And now to launch
my force-field generator,
and now to sink it.

An oracle has been expecting me,
a cat toy of the mind's clay,
a human riding on my back.
He directs me as I direct him to.

I Point at the Ceiling and Say "Snow" Even Though There Is No Snow There

Yesterday I brought some creamed corn into the sauna at
     my gym
and photographed it dripping, little by little, from the wooden
     bench

onto the wooden bench below

and then I poured a little more

and more dripped down.

No one saw me

though I left this mess
for the cleaning staff.

So someone, besides you,

must already know what I did

though I imagine they cannot picture me

or Grox.

Or my t-shirt, which depicts Grox.

Or my love.

I Cough into Your Face and You Cough into Mine

I was practicing suspending a coin in midair,
a coin the size of a standard desk globe
and the weight of a very heavy thing.

And now I remember something already ghoulish,
my majestic pink belly glowing in the dark.

The belly button ought to be sexy but isn't;
it's sexy to the one who licks it but feels
like nothing to the one who's licked,
so that both parties will eventually decide
to end the awkwardness of trading pleasure
and sit back and instead read the script
on the decorative
napkins they've been given.

The script that says "the world is not terrible,
it's pretty awesome,"

which no one believes,
which kills all desire.

14

Once I tried to have my computer repaired. That somehow sounds old-fashioned now, but I did.

A computer repair guy came to my apartment and played around on the computer for a few hours. Then he charged me $160 and said he couldn't fix it. I felt like I had to pay him, so I paid him, and he gave me a complimentary cookie that this computer repair company would give out.

I was starving, since I'd had to wait for several hours while this guy tried to fix my computer and didn't really have any food around. I ate the cookie and lay on my bed.

The next day I felt quite ill and laid down. Then I got up suddenly and rushed to use the toilet. Then I suffered from food poisoning for about twelve hours, mostly sitting on the toilet and vomiting into the tub next to it. At some points I lay on the floor in the bathroom and vomited into the toilet, drifting in and out of sleep. I woke again coughing, trying to vomit, and realized with alarm that I was choking on whatever it was I was vomiting up. "I'm going to die on a bathroom floor," I thought. Eventually I brought up a gelatinous black mass, though I missed the toilet and coughed it straight onto the floor. It seemed to be the source of the poisoning and I decided it must be the cookie from the previous day. Why would I eat a cookie from a computer repair place that could not even fix my computer. Why would I eat that.

However, the gelatinous black mass unfurled itself and showed it was feathered. Sorry, it said to me. Sorry, it said again, I mean, your life is about to get kind of better, but the overall trajectory of the world is about to get much worse. You're probably best off if you stay here with your broken computer and vomit-covered tub.

Fuck you, I said, fuck you.

A Glimmering Corridor Invites You In

I'm sleeping in the Room of Salted Flesh
watching a garish thing,
basically a feathered woman.

Basically a feathered woman
putting on another skin.

And so I communicate to you with my vomit
altering color and texture to create a code
making my ideas as concrete as possible.

My idea is that we should go to the aquarium, the beach.

And now at the beach I watch someone pull a cigarette butt
from the nose of a sea turtle using a pliers while the sea turtle
bleeds and resists. I mean blood runs from the sea turtle's nose
while the sea turtle jerks and cries with pain. My relationship
to the sea turtle: now it's a bomb I've never dropped.

And so my eyes burrow deep within the pockets of my face.

Maybe one of you is a prison guard and the other a prisoner.
Having gone to school together, you recognize one another.
And eventually begin sleeping together. When you sleep to-
gether, you remember the smell of Pine Sol from when you
were just starting to crawl. You smell the scent of Pine Sol and
keep enjoying one another; you enjoy one another so much.
There's a third character in this stupid scene, though, too.
That character wears a t-shirt that says, "I paint so that I don't
snap." This character watches you the prisoner and you the
guard fucking. Sitting on a train, he returns to his true form,
the form of a child. He speculates to his friend: "If my family
were rich, I'd wake up in the morning and get a hundred-

dollar bill instead of a one-dollar bill."

But no one in this scene is rich, and each character stashes their money deep within their heart, so that it is no longer just a piece of paper but a continuous wave pulsing at a frequency that comes from a mysterious part of the brain.

When I see this scene a stream of water shoots out of my fingertip, freezes, and forms an ice gun. Yet despite the ice along the line of my hand, I'm sweating full force.

And when I look at the hardwood floor underneath me, my sweat has pooled, I'm slipping in it, it's forming shapes, pools the shape of children doing acrobatics. Liquid children and then my skin raising into gooseflesh, nuggets also shaped like children, terrible terrible children who speculate on what would be different if their families were rich.

And wearing my camo jacket to bed,
I dream myself out in an iron bed that folds down from the wall.
Here we are dreaming in this iron bed.

I'm sleeping in the Hammer Distro
watching myself cry in the mirror.

Here I create Powerball,
a game. Here I bend my knees, then unbend them
and trust my vicious body
to walk the earth.

Both of My Touches

I'm always great to have around, in that I want so much that I
warp the wood floors with my drool

and seeing how warped the floors are, everyone else infers my
want, copies it, and feels

nagging holes in their hearts, lack of love, lack of stuff, an ab-
sence where they'd hoped

for a feeling of pride and success.

But you.

As a retiring state employee, you can probably buy a cheap
    winter home in Florida,

if you've managed your money well. And have a yard that
    backs up to some woods,

that feels very private. If you're particularly lucky, you can
    probably end up on the edge

of the subdivision and feel like your home is even more
    private.

And this is a good deal, a good investment.

All yours, and you can drool with a mixture of satisfaction

and a deeper want, a want that you couldn't even really
    fathom

if you didn't have this winter home in Florida,

if you were someone else or had done things a bit differently,

a bit more poorly.

This drool can capture both want and deep satisfaction at
    your ability

to feel this particular kind of want

as you walk around your private

house, your house with so much privacy,

drooling and drooling.

Letting it drip

from your mouth
down to your chin
and drop down
onto the floor
which isn't
covered in cat hair,
which has been
swept pretty recently,
which is ready
to receive
your drool.

Later you can see it
and dab at it with a Kleenex.

Or maybe just let it go
and walk over it for a few hours,

and it won't be there anymore.

Though in that scenario there is a point
at which you stop salivating.

And that point definitely doesn't exist.

Sometimes in the dead of night

I wake up to find my tongue's become a thin metal rod

because the meat of the tongue fell off, and that's what was left

so everyone will know that I've always had a tongue

that's a thin metal rod underneath.

A rod unsuited to drinking beers, eating hot dogs,

or even talking to cool or interesting women, much less
    being one,

much less looking at myself in the mirror

and seeing both a cool, interesting woman and the kind of
    girl or guy

who could pick up a cool, interesting woman, or, you know,

who could go to a show on a warm Saturday with someone
    new and cute

and have a good time and not think about their drool

or their parents' drool or even their friends' drool.

Instead I'm the type of person who would, as soon as they'd
stopped drooling,

eat part of a sandwich from a very legit-seeming Italian place

and immediately puke into a trash can

about 10 seconds after telling a chatty stranger how great
the sandwich is.

That's the kind of thing I would do.

ROOF BOOKS
the best in language since 1976

Recent & Selected Titles

• BOOK ABT FANTASY by Chris Sylvester. 104 p. $16.95

• NOISE IN THE FACE OF by David Buuck. 104 p. $16.95

• FRANKLINSTEIN by Susan Landers. 144 p. $16.95

• PLATO'S CLOSET by Lawrence Giffin. 144 p. $16.95

• PARSIVAL by Steve McCaffery. 88 p. $15.95

• DEAD LETTER by Jocelyn Saidenberg. 94 p. $15.95

• social patience by David Brazil. 136 p. $15.95

• THE PHOTOGRAPHER by Ariel Goldberg. 84 p. $15.95

• TOP 40 by Brandon Brown. 138 p. $15.95

• THE MEDEAD by Fiona Templeton. 314 p. $19.95

• LYRIC SEXOLOGY VOL. 1 by Trish Salah. 138 p. $15.95

• INSTANT CLASSIC by erica kaufman. 90 p. $14.95

• A MAMMAL OF STYLE by Kit Robinson
& Ted Greenwald. 96 p. $14.95

• VILE LILT by Nada Gordon. 114 p. $14.95

• DEAR ALL by Michael Gottlieb. 94 p. $14.95

• FLOWERING MALL by Brandon Brown. 112 p. $14.95.

• MOTES by Craig Dworkin. 88 p. $14.95

• APOCALYPSO by Evelyn Reilly. 112 p. $14.95

• BOTH POEMS by Anne Tardos. 112 p. $14.95

Roof Books are published by
Segue Foundation
300 Bowery • New York, NY 10012
For a complete list, please visit **roofbooks.com**

Roof Books are distributed by
SMALL PRESS DISTRIBUTION
1341 Seventh Street • Berkeley, CA. 94710-1403.
spdbooks.org